What Is The Bible?

Finding Our Place in God's Story

Jared M. August

What Is the Bible?
Finding Our Place in God's Story
Copyright © 2021 by Jared M. August

Published by Northeastern Baptist Press
               Post Office Box 4600
               Bennington, VT 05201

All rights reserved. No part of this book may be reproduced in any form without prior permission from Northeastern Baptist Press, except as provided for by USA copyright law.

Scripture quotations are from The Holy Bible, English Standard Version® (ESV®), copyright © 2001 by Crossway Bibles, a publishing ministry of Good News Publishers. Used by permission. All rights reserved.

Paperback ISBN: 978-1-953331-05-2
ePub ISBN: 978-1-953331-07-6

To Larry and Lisa Tompkins,
for asking "so what?"

Your word is a lamp to my feet
and a light to my path.

Psalm 119:105

Table of Contents

Introduction	i
1 The Bible is the story...	1
2 ...of God's work...	17
3 ...to destroy evil...	33
4 ...restore creation...	51
5 ...and dwell with his people forever.	71
6. So what?	89
Endnotes	100

Introduction

As he stood at the stake, a gaunt and exhausted William Tyndale was offered one final chance: Recant or die. After eighteen months in prison, the forty-two-year-old Tyndale opened his mouth and cried, "Lord, open the King of England's eyes." With that, the noose tightened and England lost one of the greatest reformers the world has ever known. His crime? He translated the Bible into the language of the people, into English. Tyndale believed so strongly in the importance of the Bible that he gave his life so others could read it.

This book exists to answer one question: *What is the Bible?* While this might seem an odd question to ask—and perhaps an even more odd title for a book—the answer to this question affects every aspect of the Christian faith. Although some may find this question simplistic, anyone who has spent anytime reading the Bible knows the complexities involved with attempting an answer.

So again, *What is the Bible?* Of course we can provide any number of "correct" answers: The Word of

God, the Holy Scriptures, the Christian life map, the books of the Old and New Testaments, and the list goes on. All of these answers are correct. But what is it all about? What makes it different? What gives it authority? What makes it worth dying for? What *is* it?

This question is further complicated when one considers the nature of the Bible. The book we call the Bible is really an anthology of sixty-six books, divided into two sections—thirty-nine in what we call the Old Testament and twenty-seven in what we call the New Testament. It was written by over forty authors—ranging from fishermen to kings, from servants to government officials, from poor exiles to wealthy business owners, and from farmers to tax collectors. It was penned on three continents—Europe, Asia, and Africa—over a time period of at least fifteen-hundred years in three different languages. Can something so diverse really have any unity?

In the pages that follow, we seek to answer the question "What is the Bible?" by considering how Scripture recounts a story—*our* story. In this story, God is the Author. He is the one who has given promises; he is the one who will reign victorious in the end. In this story, God gives us the invitation to participate. We are offered the chance to join in, to live by faith in the promises of the Lord.

INTRODUCTION

To be honest, this book is quite simple. In fact, it can be summarized in just one sentence (as the chapters indicate!). My hope is that by reading it, you may grasp afresh the exhilarating reality that as believers in Jesus, our lives are woven into the very fabric of God's story. As we ponder the many puzzle pieces of the Bible, we come face to face with a unified and beautiful picture. Despite its diversity, the unity of its hope is overwhelming.

My sincere desire is that by considering our story anew, we come away with greater appreciation for the Author. In the end, we look to the one who, some fifteen hundred years prior to Tyndale's confession, stood similarly gaunt and exhausted. He too was offered one final chance: recant or die. But on the eve of his rigged midnight trial, the thirty three-year old Nazarene opened his mouth and cried, "Not my will but yours." With that, the betrayer arrived, the trial commenced, and the nails were struck. The world watched as its Maker bowed his head. But that was not the end. In many ways, it was just the beginning. *The Bible is the story of God's work to destroy evil, restore creation, and dwell with his people forever.*

1

The Bible is the story ...

> **Story** /stohr-ee/:
> An account of events;
> A narrative with a plot or storyline

Jesus was the master storyteller. He told so many stories and parables that at one point, his disciples actually came and asked him why (Matthew 13:10). One occasion in particular always catches my attention.

Luke 24:13-35

In this passage, two disciples, Cleopas and his friend, are leaving Jerusalem after their Leader's crucifixion. It had been three and a half years since Jesus began his public ministry. During that time, countless individuals had listened with anticipation to what Jesus taught. They hung on his every word. They believed he was the long-awaited Savior whom the Scriptures had prophesied. They believed he would set them free from Roman bondage. They believed he would provide freedom to captives and joy to the brokenhearted. But then he died.

Just one week after his Triumphal Entry, Jesus was betrayed by one of his own, unjustly tried by the religious leaders, and executed upon a Roman cross. Clearly these two disciples are disappointed. They are surprised, confused, and unsure of what to believe.

But as they trudge towards the village of Emmaus, the resurrected Jesus appears to them. Although they don't recognize him, he comes alongside them and starts asking questions. In this fascinating conversation, Jesus asks what they are discussing. They describe the events from the past week—how they had hoped that this Jesus of Nazareth would be the one to redeem Israel (not realizing that they are talking to him!). Jesus waits patiently for them to explain the whole situation. And then he responds. His response is nothing short of amazing:

> O foolish ones, and slow of heart to believe all that the prophets have spoken! Was it not necessary that the Christ should suffer these things and enter into his glory? (Luke 24:25–26).

What does Jesus do next? He tells them a story:

> And beginning with Moses and all the Prophets, he interpreted to them in all

> the Scriptures the things concerning himself (24:27).

Jesus doesn't just tell them any story. He tells them *the* story. He tells them the story of the Bible. And evidently, he does so in a rather engaging way. When they reach the village after walking for hours with Jesus, they beg him to come and have dinner with them. They can't get enough of this story.

Jesus agrees to spend the evening with these disciples in their village. At dinner, Jesus takes the bread, blesses it, breaks it, and allows their eyes to be opened. Instantly they recognize him, and he vanishes. Then we read this incredible verse:

> They said to each other, "Did not our hearts burn within us while he talked to us on the road, while he opened to us the Scriptures?" (24:32).

Did not our hearts burn within us?

Let me ask, when was the last time our hearts burned within us when we read the Bible? When was the last time we simply couldn't put it down? Do we ever lose track of time while meditating on Scripture? Do we ever exclaim intense appreciation and extravagant praise for God's Word, like the author of Psalm 119?

> My soul is consumed with longing for your rules at all times (119:20).

> The law of your mouth is better to me than thousands of gold and silver pieces (119:72).
>
> Oh how I love your law! It is my meditation all the day (119:97).
>
> How sweet are your words to my taste, sweeter than honey to my mouth! (119:103).

Now don't get me wrong, the goal of this book is not to guilt anyone into manufacturing these emotions. On the contrary, my hope is that we might realize afresh the unique nature of the Bible as our story. The Bible is certainly God's story, yet when we embrace God as the Author of all things, we can claim it as our story too.

I believe that if we spend more time meditating on this reality, it will cause us to better grasp the implications of the Bible and to truly appreciate its claims. Just as the hearts of the disciples on the road to Emmaus "burned within them," when we grasp the Bible as not just *a* story, but *our* story, our hearts will inevitably burn with joy within us as well.

Our Story Versus *A* Story

When my wife and I began to get to know each other, we often wrote letters—good, old-fashioned, pen and paper letters. For a while, we wrote a letter every single day. We saved these letters, and every now and again we pull out the box to read through a few and reflect on what we wrote.

To be honest, each letter can be understood completely by itself. Not that you'd want to read them, but if you were to do so, you could easily determine our exact intended meaning. In fact, if you really wanted to, you could probably read them all. You could trace the main themes. You could parse all the verbs and diagram all the sentences. You could even set them to music and memorize the important lines! You could know them inside and out.

Yet these letters have *dramatically* different implications for me. While yes, of course the meaning would be identical whether you read them or I read them, the significance is drastically different. See, these letters are part of *my* story. These letters were addressed to *me*. The content is relevant to *my* life. I experienced the events described in them. I love the one who wrote them.

We have the same situation with the Bible, don't we? We can parse all the verbs and diagram all the sentences; we can set parts to music and memorize the important verses. We can know it inside and out.

However, the Bible has dramatically different implications for those of us who bear the title *Child of God* than it does for those who do not. For those of us who are believers in Jesus Christ, this is *our* story. We embrace these letters as messages for *us*. Yes, they were written thousands of years ago, but they were divinely intended for *our* benefit. They describe the one who loves us and who gave his life for us.

In accounts such as Luke 24 and Psalm 119, it is clear that these individuals embraced God's revelation as *their* story. While they of course understood Scripture as fact, they didn't take it as *just* fact. They interpreted it as the story into which their lives perfectly fit.

When we say the Bible is a story, by no means do we diminish its historical accuracy. On the contrary, it is only when we realize that the Bible is the one true story that we more deeply appreciate its claims upon our lives. It is certainly true that all people (both those who believe and those who do not believe) are already part of this story. However, it is only when we embrace God's story as our story, that we are offered a confident future expectation. When we embrace this reality, we are offered the chance to live "by faith" in the promises of God.

Just as the two disciples on the road to Emmaus experienced their hearts burning within them, and just as the psalmist overflowed with passion for God's Word, we too can experience this same hope.

The Bible Provides The Way To Know God

Before we can truly grasp the joyful new situation the Emmaus-bound disciples experienced, we must first identify their original disappointment. Why were they sad?

Consider how they responded when Jesus inquired about their intense conversation. Notice the reason for their disappointment:

> Concerning Jesus of Nazareth, a man who was a prophet mighty in deed and word before God and all the people, and how our chief priests and rulers delivered him up to be condemned to death, and crucified him. But we had hoped that he was the one to redeem Israel (24:19–21).

These disciples think they are speaking to an uninformed stranger. He lacks information. They explain recent events to the resurrected Lord Jesus. They believed Jesus of Nazereth was "a prophet mighty in deed." They recount the horrors leading up to his death—how the religious rulers had condemned him and crucified him. Yet they then provide one vital piece of information about their disillusioned faith: "We had hoped that he was the one to redeem Israel."

Not "we hope," but "we had hoped." Although they had previously believed that Jesus was the promised Christ—the long-awaited Savior of the Old Testament—upon his death, they lost that faith. It was not until Jesus reminded them of the intrinsically anticipatory nature of the Old Testament and how it all pointed to the events which had transpired that weekend in Jerusalem, that they were finally refreshed and renewed in spirit.

These disciples had longed for the story of Scripture to be true; they had longed for the metanarrative of the Bible to be fulfilled in the life of Jesus of Nazareth. Yet it took Jesus' recounting of the hope of the Bible to encourage their hearts and instill a fresh anticipation of what was to come.

In the pages that follow, we briefly trace the storyline of the Bible. As we do, we will better understand the hopes and desires of these disciples.

Creation

Genesis 1–2 describes God's magnificent creation of the universe. As he progressively calls into existence and fashions all things—from rolling pastures to rocky mountains, from billowing seas to starlit skies—the text records, "God saw that it was good" (1:4, 10, 12, 18, 21, 25, 31). In this pristine new world, God freely dwells with the people he created—Adam and Eve (3:8–9). Everything is good. Everyone is at peace. This is the way God intended it to be.

De-Creation

Genesis 3 provides a glimpse into the downward spiral of humanity. The serpent—who is later revealed to be Satan—appears and tempts Adam and Eve to disobey God's only command. After succumbing to the serpent's temptation and partaking of the forbidden fruit (2:17; 3:6), Adam and Eve's eyes are opened (3:7) and their relationship with the Lord is severed (3:8–13). Subsequently, the Lord describes the curse brought upon the world:

> Cursed is the ground because of you ...
> for you are dust, and to dust you shall
> return (3:17b, 19b).

Adam and Eve are banished from the Garden where God dwelt with them. As the universe plummets into chaos, death now reigns; disease, hunger, and sadness are ever present realities. Perhaps most importantly, humanity is no longer innocent before the Lord. This is the world in which we now live.

New Creation Promised

Despite Adam and Eve's rebellion against God's plan, out of his goodness and mercy, the Lord refuses to leave humanity without hope. In the midst of the curse upon the serpent, he proclaims a clear promise:

> I will put enmity between you and the woman, and between your offspring and her offspring; he shall bruise your head, and you shall bruise his heel (3:15).

In this promise, Adam and Eve are given the hope of a future Descendant who will defeat the serpent. Once this serpent (the anti-God, tempting, evil and rebellious one) is defeated and the world rid of its influence, God is able to reconcile with his people and restore the world to the way it was intended, the Genesis 1-2 state. Throughout the Old Testament, this promise of restoration is confirmed and clarified.

Through individuals such as Noah (5:29), Shem (9:26-27), Abraham (12:1-3; 22:16-18), Isaac (26:3-5), Jacob (28:13-14), Judah (49:10), and David (2 Samuel 7:8-17), the Lord provides promises reconfirming the hope of this promised Skull-Crushing, Creation-Restoring Descendant. The prophets unanimously testify to the future coming of an individual (referred to as the "Messiah," the "Servant of the Lord," the "Son of David") who will one day destroy evil, restore creation, and enable God to once again dwell with his people. The fact that the Old Testament does not distinguish between the Messiah's first and second coming was a source of confusion for many first-century believers.

New Creation Realized

Ultimately, it was the hope of every believing Israelite that God would one day cataclysmically judge the world and bring salvation to his people. In one sense, this event would mark the end of the world. Yet in another, it would mark the beginning. The Israelites' hope was in a physical resurrection and eventual establishment of the new heavens and new earth (Isaiah 65:17).

They eagerly anticipated the "Day of the Lord" in which God would bring about the fulfillment of the promises given to the patriarchs. The prophet Daniel was given a vision of what this would entail:

> I saw in the night visions, and behold, with the clouds of heaven there came one like a son of man, and he came to the Ancient of Days and was presented before him. And to him was given dominion and glory and a kingdom, that all peoples, nations, and languages should serve him; his dominion is an everlasting dominion, which shall not pass away, and his kingdom one that shall not be destroyed (Daniel 7:13–14).

In this coming eschatological kingdom, the Israelites believed that God would fully dwell with his people for the first time since Eden. This time, however, paradise would last forever. No longer would a barrier be necessary between God and man, as in the tabernacle and temple. No longer would evil reign. God would forgive iniquity and remember sin no more. The Israelites longed for the day when they could experience unhindered fellowship with their Creator once again.

Throughout the sequence *Creation*, *De-Creation*, *New Creation Promised*, and *New Creation Realized*, the consistent hope was and is that through the Chosen Servant, God would destroy evil, restore creation, and dwell with his people. The hope was always in God's promise to fix all things and bring the world back to the way it was intended—the Genesis 1–2 "very good" state. While the circumstances of God's people continually shifted, God's promise remained secure. This is where the Emmaus-bound disciples found themselves—struggling to hold on to the hope of God's story.

This is also where we find ourselves. Our circumstances are quite different from those of the Emmaus disciples some two thousand years ago. We too long for God's Chosen Servant, Jesus Christ, to destroy evil and restore creation so that God can once again physically dwell with his people.

Just as they had, we also struggle with the brutal results of sin. We yearn for the day when the Savior will come "with the clouds of heaven" and fix this broken world. Until then, we stand shoulder to shoulder with God's redeemed from throughout the ages. We stand side by side with Abraham and

Moses, Rahab and Ruth, David and Daniel, as we eagerly await the conclusion of God's story.

Putting The Facts Where They Belong

As we engage the text of the Bible as one unified story, it would serve us well to continually consider the reality of the Bible as *our* story. Surprisingly, even in our largely secular culture, seventy-one percent of Americans regard the Bible as the Word of God. Fifty-five percent go so far as to claim that it is without error.[1] These numbers are striking. Out of every ten Americans, seven of them view the Bible as God's Word!

Yet I cannot help but wonder, how many embrace the Bible as *their* story? Yes, perhaps they recognize that there is something special about the Bible. Perhaps they have seen lives changed by it. Perhaps they have even read it for themselves. But have they accepted *its* hope as *their* hope?

An unfortunate aspect of our modern culture is our preoccupation with compartmentalization. This is often evident even with our theology textbooks. We divide them into "doctrines"—maybe ten or twelve, maybe more or less. Although these textbooks are vital in helping us comprehend the facts of our faith, all too often they leave the impression that the Bible is merely a list of facts. Of course the Bible is a record of historical events and facts. Yet on the other hand, it is so much more. It is our hope!

Apart from understanding the Bible as one unified story, we are left with the impression that it has no rising action, no plot twists, no climax, and no resolution. We certainly notice startling details and fascinating narratives as we read various accounts about Noah's ark, David and Goliath, or Paul and his missionary journeys. Yet what's often missed is how these many stories make up one unified story. Again, if you've ever picked up a theology textbook, you surely know what I mean. Flip through the pages and you'll find incredible truths about Christology, Theology Proper, and Eschatology. But unless we first embrace the unified narrative of Scripture as our story, it is difficult to grasp the relevancy of many of these facts.

Again, don't get me wrong. I love theology. I love these facts. My intent is not to diminish theology, but to elevate it. For once we embrace the Bible as our story, all these facts and details matter *so much more*. Every doctrine, from the inerrancy of Scripture to the virgin birth of Jesus Christ, begins to take on a whole new meaning. No longer are these facts viewed as merely details of ancient events, rather, they are understood as realities of our story.

Here's the point: I believe that if we embrace the Bible as the grand-metanarrative of history—

the story into which our lives uniquely fit—we will be far better equipped to handle whatever circumstances life may throw at us. If God's promise of restoration is understood as the ultimate conclusion to our story, then all the adventures and all the pains, all the joys and all the sorrows, all the laughter and all the tears, will consistently point us back to the very same hope that caused the hearts of the Emmaus-bound disciples to burn within them, the very same hope that has been offered from Genesis through Revelation.

The Bible is the story ...

Chapter 1 Discussion Questions:

1. How is the story of the Bible different than other stories?

2. As discussed above, a rather high percentage of Americans (71%) regard the Bible as the Word of God. How might we encourage these individuals to live by faith?

3. Many in our culture are searching for *meaning* and *purpose* in life. Can you think of some examples?

4. What difference does embracing the Bible as "our story" practically make in our lives?

5. What is your story (testimony) and how does it fit into God's story?

2

... of God's work ...

The Bible contains the accounts of hundreds of people who lived over the course of thousands of years. Consider how the following accounts relate to each other and what each of them have in common: Noah's construction of an unusually large boat, Abraham's migration from his homeland to a country unknown, Jochebed's making of a floating basket for her infant son Moses, Rahab's concealing of the two Israelite spies, Ruth's commitment to follow Naomi's God, David's slaying of Goliath, Daniel's devotion to prayer no matter the cost, Joseph's obedience in marrying a pregnant woman, Peter's gospel proclamation while imprisoned, and Paul's testimony when shipwrecked.

Clearly, this is just a brief selection of actions by individuals recorded in the Bible. Countless other acts of faith are found throughout Scripture. In every case, by demonstrating faith through action, the individual follows, obeys, and serves the Lord.

Yet despite the diversity of these acts of faith, in every case the *hope* of the individual was the same. When each of these situations are examined, it becomes evident that despite the dramatic differences, each individual had placed his or her faith in God as the Author and Founder of creation and restoration.

In the pages that follow, the topic of "God's work" is examined. Since the Bible is our story, we discuss what it means that God is the Author. Through considering the creation account of Genesis 1–2, the fall of Genesis 3, and the promise of restoration in Genesis 3:15, it becomes evident that from the beginning, God's promise to his people has been strikingly consistent.

In light of the promise first given in Genesis 3:15 and progressively developed throughout the rest of Scripture, the hope of God's destruction of evil, restoration of creation, and future dwelling with his people is revealed as the central hope of the redeemed people of God throughout the ages.

Author of Creation

From the very beginning of the Bible, God is revealed as the Author of all. In Genesis chapters one and two, the Lord creates the heavens and the earth. As he creates the universe, the text records that after each day, "God saw that it was good" (1:4, 10, 12, 18, 21, 25). In fact, upon completion of creation, the text records that it was "*very* good" (1:31).

All of creation is brought into existence simply because God *speaks* it into existence. At the beginning of each day (and many times in between) the text records, "And God said ..." (1:3, 6, 9, 11, 14, 20, 24, 26, 28, 29). In each case, the point is that God—the all-powerful Ruler of creation and Author of all things—must simply speak to accomplish his goal. Think about that. God speaks, the world obediently responds.

But we can go further than that, can't we? Since God creates the universe out of nothing, his words are infinitely powerful. Compare this with what we often refer to as our "creations." I think of wood-working. There is something greatly rewarding about taking a plank of pine and turning it into a sturdy bookshelf or a decorative table. Some love painting—taking a blank white canvas and adding just the right shade of just the right color at just the right time. Others enjoy sculpting, sewing, knitting, or poetry. Yet no matter how inspiring the poem, how breath-taking the portrait, or how solid the furniture, all these "creations" are in an entirely different category than God's creation.

Although countless distinctions could be drawn between God's creation and our creations, the one that is perhaps most amazing is that God uses *nothing* to make *something*. God simply proclaims, "Let there be light" (1:3) and there suddenly is light. He announces, "Let the earth sprout vegetation" (1:11) and plants begin to grow. He declares, "Let the earth bring forth living creatures" (1:24) and the animals come into existence. All God must do is communicate something in order for it to happen. Unlike us, he does not need watercolors and a paintbrush, or nails and a hammer to construct his masterpiece.

And then we come to God's creation of man and woman. Although God could have simply spoken them into existence, in this case, he chose to personally form Adam and Eve in a way distinct from all other creatures:

> Then the Lord God formed the man of dust from the ground and breathed into his nostrils the breath of life, and the man became a living creature (2:7).

Just as a potter forms his clay, the Lord God fashions Adam out of the dust of the ground. Since there is no "helper fit" for Adam (2:18), the Lord carefully fashions a perfect match, Eve (2:21–23).

Furthermore, in 1:27, we learn that God created man and woman "in the image of God." In other words, Adam and Eve are made distinct; they are fashioned to reflect many of the characteristics (what theologians have called "communicable attributes") of the Creator. For example, just as God is holy, righteous, just, fair, loving, caring, and compassionate, Adam and Eve are able to emulate these qualities in their rulership over the world.

This reality places them—and us!—in a category completely distinct from all animals. We do not exist merely to survive, rather, we exist to fellowship with God and to extend his rule over his creation. This is especially evident in the commission given to this first couple by the Lord:

> Be fruitful and multiply and fill the earth and subdue it and have dominion over the fish of the sea and over the birds of the heavens and over every living thing that moves on the earth (1:28).

In this first commission, Adam and Eve are given the command to expand God's influence wherever they go upon the earth.

Not only are Adam and Eve (and by extension, all humanity) entrusted with care of creation, but they are also given the opportunity for unique fellowship and communion with their Creator which no other creature can experience in quite the same way. Even in this commission, the Lord God *speaks* with this couple; he *communicates* with them and informs them that he will provide for their needs. He announces that "every plant yielding seed" and "every tree with seed in its fruit" will be for their food (1:29). They shall not hunger. They shall not lack. They shall not suffer. They shall not worry. Their God will meet all their needs.

The Lord even provides Adam and Eve with their home, the Garden of Eden. The text states:

> And the Lord God planted a garden in Eden, in the east, and there he put the man whom he had formed (2:8).

Truly, this couple is given a paradise unparalleled. They are given each other, they are provided sustenance, they experience perfect communion with their Creator, and they can enjoy a beautiful place in which to dwell. They receive only one prohibition by the Lord:

> Of the tree of the knowledge of good and evil you shall not eat, for in the day that you eat of it you shall surely die (2:17).

Adam and Eve are given everything they could ever want. There is just one stipulation: *Don't eat the fruit.*

About this prohibition, some wonder, "What's the big deal with the fruit? Why does God care so much about what Adam and Eve can and cannot eat?"

While perhaps this is an intriguing question, it misses the focus of this passage. The point is that God essentially says, "I'm going to give you everything you could ever need, anything you could ever want. *But*, you still need to acknowledge me as God.

You must recognize that I am the Creator and King of the universe. You must realize that I know what is best. You must choose to trust me as your Provider and Sustainer."

If we just focus on the fruit, we miss the entire point. Quite simply, the fruit is not what matters. What matters is Adam's heart—what matters is whether or not Adam and Eve will trust God and acknowledge him as their Ruler. God has given this couple everything imaginable, yet by posing this command, he quietly and patiently asks, "Will you *trust* me? Will you *choose* me?"

Man's Choice

We know how this story ends, don't we? What could have been an eternally happy ending turns into a painful account of the bitter results of man's rebellion. Genesis 3 records how the serpent appears to Adam and Eve and entices them to eat this forbidden fruit. They resist for a time, only to later succumb. Eve eats first, then gives some to Adam. Upon consuming this fruit, "the eyes of both were opened, and they knew that they were naked" (3:7).

When Adam and Eve partook of the fruit, something happened, something that could not easily be undone. They not only lost their innocence, but every part of them—their emotions, will, and mind—became corrupted by sin. No longer would they naturally seek God's will. From this point on, they would seek their own will. Theologians refer to this event as "the fall" and the result as humanity's "depravity."

Whereas before, the holy and perfect Creator God could dwell in intimate fellowship with Adam and Eve, as a result of their choice, this relationship with God is severed. Adam and Eve made their choice and thereby defiantly raised their fist against their Maker.

At this point, we must consider the identity of the serpent. In light of its supernatural ability to speak—and thereby tempt—Adam and Eve must have recognized a difference between this snake and any other snake. Although the New Testament identifies the serpent as "Satan" (Revelation 20:2), Adam and Eve would have been unable to do so. However, they certainly would have been able to perceive its abnormality among the other animals. About this, the text states:

> Now the serpent was more crafty than any beast of the field which the Lord God had made (3:1).

Although the serpent is never explicitly called "evil" in Genesis, in light of: (1) its ability to tempt, (2) the resultant curse brought upon creation, (3) the undoing of what God had declared "good," (4) its status as "crafty," and (5) the New Testament's reference to it as the "devil" and "evil" (e.g., John 8:44; 1 John 3:12), it certainly seems that "evil one" is an appropriate and fitting title.[2]

As a result of Adam and Eve's rejection and rebellion against the Lord, the universe descends into chaos. In 3:14-19, the Lord declares the curse brought upon the world and its horrific consequences:

> Cursed is the ground because of you ...
> for you are dust, and to dust you shall
> return (3:17b, 19b).

No longer can man and woman dwell in the presence of their Creator. No longer can they experience perfect harmony together. No longer are they given all they could ever need. And no longer are they able to cultivate the ground with ease (2:5). Now thorns and thistles will grow (3:18); the earth will rebel against man just as man rebelled against God.

Spiritual death (separation of the soul from God) is already a reality, and physical death (separation of the soul from the body) is not far behind. Everything that previously was declared "good," now begins to crumble. God's creation is no longer as it was designed to be. This is the world in which we live today.

Although each of us experience the bitter results of the curse in different ways, we all have tasted it in one form or another. Everyone has experienced sickness, pain, and loss. All have sinned against God, and—unless the Lord returns—every single one of us will experience death.

Harsh, you may think? Possibly. At least it feels that way. Yet honestly, one of the undeniably verifiable aspects of our faith is the reality of the curse. If you look around at the world in which we live, you will come face to face with suffering and hurting people. In many ways, the curse is what every single person in this world cannot help but fight against. No one wants to get sick. No one wants to experience betrayal. No one wants to be rejected. No one wants to die.

And we can go further, too. The results of the curse are seen in the nature of every single person. No one needs to be taught how to be selfish, nobody needs to be shown how to lie, and no one needs to learn how to hate, covet, or lust. The natural "sinfulness" of man is self evident. Subsequent to the fall, every single person is born at odds with God. The apostle Paul states this clearly when he writes that apart from God's mercy, we are God's enemies (Romans 5:10).

The incredible reality of the curse is that it levels the playing field. For the Christian who wonders how he can relate to an unbeliever to share the gospel, the answer is actually quite simple: *start with the curse*. Every individual in this world—the conservative and the liberal, the Christian and the Muslim, the rich and the poor, the young and the old—has an intrinsic knowledge that this world is not as it should be. That is why we find so many people fighting for so many causes.

Although many causes are noble and good, in every case, the only final solution is found in Scripture. For outside of the divine hope offered by God, nothing else can satisfy.

Author of Restoration

Ultimately, the only hope and solution to this dire situation is offered by God, for he is the Author of restoration. As discussed in the previous chapter, in Genesis 3:15, God proclaims to the serpent in the presence of Adam and Eve:

> I will put enmity between you and the woman, and between your offspring and her offspring; he shall bruise your head, and you shall bruise his heel.

This passage is rightfully referred to as the *protoevangelium* ("first gospel") and offers a glimmer of hope in an otherwise hopeless situation. Despite its brevity, it stands as the fountainhead from which the many promises of God flow.

Here, God promises that Adam and Eve's "Offspring" (that is, their future "Descendant") will one day crush the serpent's head. Let's consider what this entails.

As previously discussed, the serpent is no ordinary snake. He is "crafty" and well considered the "evil one." Just as God is the Author of all that is good, in many ways, the serpent is the author of that which is bad. Again, although Adam and Eve did not know its identity as Satan, this promise makes it clear that their Descendant would one day defeat the serpent and its "offspring" in some sort of battle.

Although there is debate about who is to be included in the serpent's "offspring" (Jesus later indicates in John 8:44 that it includes all those who fight against the Lord), Adam and Eve could have concluded that at the very least, it included the serpent's influence upon the world. In this way, Adam and Eve were promised that the defeat of the serpent would include the destruction of evil. In view of the context of Genesis 1–2 and the previously perfect state, it was made clear to them that this future Descendant's victory would accomplish something great.

For once the serpent is defeated, all the effects of the curse—sin, sickness, death, and pain—can be eradicated. Once the serpent is defeated, God can restore the world and bring it back to the Genesis 1-2 "very good" state. Once the serpent is defeated—and the barrier between God and man is broken—God can once again dwell in perfect communion and fellowship with his people.

Given the context of Genesis 3:15, Adam and Eve are presented with the promise that God will: (1) *Destroy evil* (by defeating the serpent and ridding the world of its influence, including all sinful acts and guilt accumulated by humanity); (2) *Restore creation* (to the Genesis 1-2 "very good" state); and (3) *Allow God to dwell with his people* (in the same way he previously dwelt with Adam and Eve). Perhaps the great reformer Martin Luther summarizes this promise best:

> Look to Adam and Eve ... because they hear the promise concerning the Seed who will crush the serpent's head, they have the same hope we have, namely, that death will be taken away, that sin will be abolished, and that righteousness, life, peace, etc., will be restored. In this hope our first parents live and die, and because of this hope they are truly holy and righteous. Thus we also live in the same hope.[3]

Luther's quote could not be more clear. The point of Genesis 3:15 is that Adam and Eve were given the promise of future restoration. They were given the hope that despite all the suffering and heartache they would endure, in the end, God would reign victorious and restore the world to the way it was intended to be.

It is this promise that serves as the basis of the rest of Scripture. All one must do is read the very next verse after the curse to discover the response of Adam and Eve to this hope:

> The man called his wife's name Eve, because she was the mother of all living (3:20).

This is the first time the woman's name is mentioned in this account. The name "Eve" sounds quite similar to the Hebrew word "Life." Furthermore, the explanation as to why her name is "Eve" is offered: "because she was the mother of all living."

Upon learning about their imminent death and the fact that they "shall return to dust," why would Adam name his wife "Life"? Adam hears his death sentence (3:19), and exclaims, "this woman is the mother of life!" (3:20). I can't help but believe that this is intentional. Adam hears the curse of death (3:16–19), yet acknowledges the promise of life (3:15), and therefore responds accordingly. He knows that it will be through the woman, through Eve, that the Skull-Crushing, Creation-Restoring Descendant will come and will accomplish that which was promised.

The Promise

As the story of the Bible progressively unfolds, this same promise continues: through the promised Descendant, God will (1) destroy evil, (2) restore creation, and (3) dwell with his people. This truth is revealed and confirmed over and over again. In fact, that is what the rest of this book is about!

This same promise is presented in various forms to Noah, Abraham, Moses, Rahab, Ruth, David, Daniel, Joseph, Peter, and Paul (and obviously, the list goes on and on). All the actions mentioned earlier involve the faith response to God and to his promises.

Although none of these Old Testament saints could articulate the identity of the promised Descendant, we can. His name is Jesus. He is the Christ, the Messiah, the Suffering Servant, the Davidic King, the Prophet after Moses, the Son of Abraham, the Offspring of Woman, the Savior, the Redeemer, and the Restorer.

And what is most encouraging of all? This same miraculous promise offered in Genesis 3:15 is the same promise that is offered to you!

The Bible is the story of God's work ...

Chapter 2 Discussion Questions:

1. Why is Genesis 3:15 such an important verse?

2. How does the book of Genesis serve as the basis for the Great Commission of Matthew 28?

3. How are our "acts of faith" similar, yet different from those of Old Testament believers?

4. What does it mean that God is the Author of creation and restoration? How should this affect one's outlook on life?

5. What are some practical ways in which we can participate in God's work?

3

... to destroy evil ...

Throughout the Gospels, Jesus is often found at the center of controversies. Most of these are with the religious leaders, who are at best, skeptical of his ministry. In Luke 18, Jesus recounts the parable of the Pharisee and the tax collector. In this illustration, Jesus contrasts the self-righteous with those whom God counts as righteous:

> Two men went up into the temple to pray, one a Pharisee and the other a tax collector. The Pharisee, standing by himself, prayed thus: "God, I thank you that I am not like other men, extortioners, unjust, adulterers, or even like this tax collector. I fast twice a week; I give tithes of all that I get." But the tax collector, standing far off, would not even lift up his eyes to heaven, but beat his breast, saying, "God, be merciful to me, a sinner!" I tell you, this man went down to his house justified, rather than the other. For everyone who exalts himself will be humbled, but the one

> who humbles himself will be exalted (18:10–14).

In this fascinating parable, the one who expects to be justified by God is not, and the one who knows he does not deserve to be justified by God is.

This is even more interesting given the religious beliefs of the Pharisees at the time. As a Pharisee, this man would have known the Scriptures word for word. He would have had vast portions committed to memory and would have been able to explain the plan of God throughout the ages. Even more ironic is the fact that as a Pharisee, he would have been able to articulate the expectation of God's future destruction of evil.

That is, he would have been able to carefully explain how the Lord God would one day return, defeat the evil one and remove his influence from creation, just as was first promised in Genesis 3:15. This Pharisee would have longed for the day when sin, sickness, and death would be eliminated and the universe restored to the way it was intended (Acts 23:8).

Yet even with this vast knowledge, he truly misses the point. In this parable, the Pharisee does not realize that he is not righteous (Psalm 14:3; 53:3), he was born a sinner (Psalm 51:5), he is naturally of the "offspring" of the evil one (John 8:44), and he deserves judgment (Psalm 7:11–12).

This brings us to the key difference between these two individuals. On the one hand, the Pharisee looks to others as his standard for righteousness: "I am not like other men." Yet on the other hand, the tax collector uses God's standard for measuring his righteousness: "Be merciful to me, a sinner!" Unlike the Pharisee, the tax collector seems to recognize that he is not righteous, that he was born a sinner, that he is naturally the "offspring" of the evil one, and that he therefore deserves judgment.

The tax collector calls out to the Lord in humble faith. He senses his need and recognizes the only one who can meet it. He begs for mercy. This is the central point of the parable: The Pharisee does not seek God's mercy, yet the tax collector does.

Even as Jesus told this parable some two thousand years ago, it is just as relevant today. Although we probably have never met anyone who identifies as a "Pharisee," I daresay there are many who hold the same attitude.

Have you ever prayed along the lines of: "*God, I thank you that I am not like other men, extortioners, unjust, adulterers, or even like this tax collector. I fast twice a week; I give tithes of all that I get*"? Many of us probably have. But let's update this list to twenty-first century language and see how practical it really is.

Have you ever prayed along the lines of: "*God, I thank you that I am not like other people who watch immoral movies and make inappropriate jokes. I go to church whenever the doors are open, all my radio presets are Christian stations, I listen to Christian podcasts every week, and I donate to many good causes"*? Or instead, do you pray, *"God, be merciful to me, a sinner!"*?

Herein lies the problem. We usually think of God's future destruction of evil as judgment of the "bad guys." While that is certainly correct, when was the last time we thought of *ourselves* as the ones who deserve judgment? When was the last time we realized that we were naturally of the "offspring of the serpent"? When was the last time we prayed like the tax collector and depended solely on the mercy of God? When was the last time we wrestled with the question of how God might effectively destroy evil without inevitably destroying us "sinners" as well?

Here's the point: It is not until we realize that we belong in the category of "bad guys" that we truly understand the holiness of God, the heart of the gospel, and the hope of man. What we discover is that the gospel allows God to defeat evil, while simultaneously forgiving all who call upon his name.

The Holiness of God

From the beginning of the Bible, God is recorded as distinct from his creation. He is completely holy and righteous. Although he had enjoyed fellowship with Adam and Eve prior to the fall, immediately after the fall he drove them out of the Garden and prohibited them from reentering (Genesis 3:24). He cannot tolerate sin in his presence.

Years later, when the Lord appears to Moses in the burning bush, he commands him, "Do not come near; take your sandals off your feet, for the place on which you are standing is holy ground" (Exodus 3:5). This holiness causes Moses to hide his face because "he was afraid to look at God" (3:6).

Later in Exodus, the Lord appears to Moses again on Mount Sinai and commands him to warn the people about coming too close to his presence on the mountain. The Lord declares the penalty:

> Whoever touches the mountain shall be put to death. No hand shall touch him, but he shall be stoned or shot; whether beast or man, he shall not live (19:12–13).

Although this warning may sound rather harsh, the Lord declares this for the *good* of the people. The Lord states, "Warn the people, lest they break through to the Lord to look and many of them perish" (19:21). The reality is that if they come too close to God's presence, they will not survive. God's holiness is too great.

As Moses continues in fellowship with the Lord, he is allowed to come closer—though never too close. In Exodus 24, the Lord allows Moses and the seventy elders of Israel to approach his presence.

Yet even this is not without significant barriers. Before they are permitted to approach the Lord, Moses offers numerous sacrifices and has the Israelites pledge complete support to the Lord (24:4–8). They are finally allowed to come before him. Yet even then, it appears that they can only see his feet:

> There was under his feet as it were a pavement of sapphire stone, like the very heaven for clearness (24:10).

Later, Moses pleads with the Lord, "Please show me your glory" (33:18). The Lord declares to Moses, "You cannot see my face, for man shall not see and live" (33:20). Yet as a result of being in his presence and seeing the physical manifestation of the backside of the Lord (33:23; 34:5), the text records that when Moses came down from the mountain, "the skin of his face shown because he had been talking with God" (34:29). This radiance was too intense for the Israelites to bear. From then on, Moses had to wear a veil over his face whenever he spoke with the Israelites (34:34). The radiance reflecting off Moses' face served as a reminder of the Lord's absolute holiness.

This same concept of God's holiness and man's inability to approach his presence is developed throughout the rest of the Bible. We find startling rules and regulations about the construction of the tabernacle and temple. We read of intricate details for ceremonial purity of the Israelites. We discover stringent requirements for the priests to offer sacrifices. It does not take long to realize that God's holiness is not something to be taken lightly.

Perhaps one of the clearest examples in all of Scripture comes from Isaiah 6. In this familiar passage, the prophet Isaiah comes face to face with the Lord upon his throne in a vision. As he gazes upon the scene, the angels proclaim in majestic procession:

> Holy, holy, holy is the Lord of hosts; the whole earth is full of his glory! (6:3).

Isaiah finds himself in the presence of the Lord God. He finds himself facing the majesty and holiness of the Author of creation, the one who formed all things. Isaiah quickly realizes that he cannot stand in the Lord's presence. His response is telling:

> Woe is me! For I am lost; for I am a man of unclean lips, and I dwell in the midst of a people with unclean lips; for my eyes have seen the King, the Lord of hosts! (6:5).

In this encounter, Isaiah recognizes the infinite difference between the Lord's holiness and his own sinfulness.

In his book, *The Holiness of God*, R. C. Sproul articulates Isaiah's situation with pointed clarity:

> For the first time in his life Isaiah really understood who God was. At the same instant, for the first time Isaiah really understood who Isaiah was. ... There was nowhere to hide. He was naked and alone before God. He had no Eve to comfort him, no fig leaves to conceal him. His was pure moral anguish, the kind that rips out the heart of a man and tears his soul to pieces. Guilt, guilt, guilt. Relentless guilt screamed from his every pore.[4]

Amazingly, Isaiah's response is quite similar to that of the tax collector in Jesus' parable, "God, be merciful to me, a sinner!" In both cases, the individual became aware of the holiness of God and thereby discovered his own depravity. He realized that he could not stand before the Lord. He recognized that apart from the Lord's mercy and grace, there was no hope. Surely Isaiah would have been familiar with the concept of God's future destruction of evil, yet it was not until this moment that he realized that apart from God's grace, this judgment would include him.

We often sing songs and talk casually about entering into the presence of the Lord. Yet I cannot help but wonder, do we really know what we are saying when we sing about entering God's presence? Do we realize that God's holiness and majesty is so great that apart from his mercy we could never stand? Do we realize that apart from his grace, we too would be included in his destruction of evil?

The Heart of the Gospel

Once it is realized that God's destruction of evil is not some obscure concept that can be relegated to "God versus the bad guys," the gospel takes on its full intended meaning. Far from revealing the Lord as a vindictive and angry Deity, his promised destruction of evil reveals his tenderness, compassion, and desire to dwell with his people. For apart from his destruction of evil, he could never again have true communion with his people, as they could never enter his presence.

Yet even here, we come back to the central dilemma: *How can God destroy evil without destroying his people?* The only solution is the cross.

It is on the cross of Jesus Christ—the promised Skull-Crushing, Creation-Restoring Descendant—that God pours out his righteous judgment upon sin. Jesus Christ becomes the substitute who bears the sin of many, so that all who call upon his name may be counted righteous before God. It is only through Jesus' sacrifice on the cross that God can count guilty, sinful people as righteous. For only once they are justified before him, can he then destroy evil without destroying them.

This expectation of a coming Messiah serves as the basis of the Old Testament hope. Consider the Suffering Servant passage of Isaiah:

> But he was pierced for our transgressions; he was crushed for our iniquities; upon him was the chastisement that brought us peace, and with his wounds we are healed. All we like sheep have gone astray; we have turned—every one—to his own way; and the Lord has laid on him the iniquity of us all. ... Out of the anguish of his soul he shall see and be satisfied; by his knowledge shall the righteous one, my servant, make many to be accounted righteous, and he shall bear their iniquities (53:5-6, 11).

In this passage, Isaiah articulates the revelation of the Lord, that the Messiah will be the one who suffers in the place of many. He will bear the penalty of mankind's rebellion and sinfulness.

Since Adam and Eve's fall, the concept of bringing God a sacrifice has been hardwired into humanity. The idea of a sacrificial offering can be found in almost every ancient (and modern) religion. Yet there is one crucial difference between what is typically taught by various religions and what is taught in Scripture.

In other religions, the sacrifice is brought to "please the gods" who demand that humans work for them. The sacrifice—be it a lamb, goat, bull, or simply an obedient life—is given to appease the gods.

Biblical sacrifice, though, is drastically different. The Scriptures teach that a sacrificial offering is given so that God might judge it in our place as our "substitute." The sacrifice dies so that the one who offered it in faith might live. Whereas the adherents of other religions offer sacrifices to work their way to God, according to the Bible, Old Testament saints offered sacrifices so that God could come to them. It's not about *man getting to God*, but rather *God getting to man*.

In other words, since the fall of Genesis 3, a sacrifice has been needed to approach the presence of the Lord. Only when an acceptable sacrifice is presented, can God place his judgment on the sacrifice rather than on the guilty man or woman. Herein lies the concept of substitution.

Fast forward to the New Testament, where the author of Hebrews discusses how Jesus is the ultimate Sacrifice for all humanity. The New Testament teaches that all the sacrifices prescribed in the Old Testament were "a shadow of the good things to come" (Hebrews 10:1), which pointed to the eventual coming of a final substitutionary sacrifice. That is, the author of Hebrews teaches that all the Old

Testament sacrifices were intrinsically anticipatory in that they were designed to draw the heart of the worshiper to recognize his own sinfulness and need for God's gracious provision of a future final sacrifice. They were intended to serve provisionally, until the coming of the Messiah:

> For since the law has but a shadow of the good things to come instead of the true form of these realities, it can never, by the same sacrifices that are continually offered every year, make perfect those who draw near. Otherwise, would they not have ceased to be offered, since the worshipers, having once been cleansed, would no longer have any consciousness of sins? But in these sacrifices there is a reminder of sins every year. For it is impossible for the blood of bulls and goats to take away sins (10:1–4).

The logic is quite clear. The "blood of bulls and goats" could never allow people to fully dwell with the Lord as he dwelt with Adam and Eve in unhindered fellowship. This is evident from even a brief survey of the Old Testament. No matter how good the sacrifice was, another was always needed soon after. Even when an acceptable sacrifice was given, due to the barriers established in the tabernacle and temple, God could still only get so close.

Yet the author of Hebrews continues in this passage to describe how Jesus—the promised Messiah and Suffering Servant of Isaiah 53—came once to offer himself as the final Sacrifice for mankind:

> And every priest stands daily at his service, offering repeatedly the same sacrifices, which can never take away sins. But when Christ had offered for all time a single sacrifice for sins, he sat down at the right hand of God, waiting from that time until his enemies should be made a footstool for his feet. For by a single offering he has perfected for all time those who are being sanctified (10:11–14).

Consider the pointed reality of this passage. Every Israelite priest for well over a thousand years was required to wake up each morning, dress in the prescribed outfit, arrive at the altar, listen to the bleating and baaing of cattle, slaughter several of these animals, burn incense, and go back home to get ready for the next day. It was a very repetitious, rather gory, and certainly messy vocation. And it never ended.

What is so astounding about this passage from Hebrews, is that Jesus "offered for all time a single sacrifice for sins" and then "sat down." The priests were not known for sitting down. They were always standing up. There was always more to be done. Always.

But not so with Jesus. As our Priest, Jesus represents us before God. As our Sacrifice, Jesus bore the penalty of God's judgment in our place. To destroy sin, God brought his judgment upon Jesus. God's only Son was crushed for *us*. He died for *us*. Why? Because God so loved the world.

Jesus did not come to merely provide an example for us to follow. He did not come merely as a "good man" to enlighten the masses. He was not just a prophet who pointed the way to God. He did not die an accidental martyr's death. Jesus lived and died as the wrath-absorbing sacrifice for the sin of mankind. Consider the following passage from Hebrews:

> Since therefore the children share in flesh and blood, he himself likewise partook of the same things, that through death he might destroy the one who has the power of death, that is, the devil, and deliver all those who through fear of death were subject to lifelong slavery (2:14–15).

These verses teach the pointed reality that Jesus' death upon the cross was the means whereby he destroyed Satan's power over death. While yes, Jesus' resurrection proves that he was victorious, it was his death on the cross that resulted in the decisive blow to the serpent.

The author of Hebrews continues by describing the implications of this event and how they impact the Christian's life:

> Therefore he had to be made like his brothers in every respect, so that he might become a merciful and faithful high priest in the service of God, to make propitiation for the sins of the people (2:17).

Although the word "propitiation" is seldom used in twenty-first century vernacular, it is a vital concept to Jesus' victory over death. The point is that Jesus became the sacrifice to pay the penalty for the sins of all humanity. Through his death, Jesus took upon himself the punishment for sin in place of all who call upon his name.

This is why the resurrection is so central to our faith. Remember that the promise from Genesis 3:15 said that the Offspring of Woman would crush the head of the serpent, yet also that the serpent would bruise the heel of the promised Offspring. The serpent would receive a mortal blow, while the Offspring would receive a minor wound. And this is exactly what happened. Jesus Christ—the Offspring of Woman—is bruised. He dies. Yet he rises again. Death cannot hold him. The serpent though, has an entirely different fate awaiting it.

This is why Christ's coming had to be in two phases. He came the first time to deal with sin, and he will come the second time to destroy evil once and for all. Consider the words from Hebrews:

> So Christ, having been offered once to bear the sins of many, will appear a second time, not to deal with sin but to save those who are eagerly waiting for him (9:28).

This Second Coming is the hope of every Christian. At this climactic event, Jesus Christ will crush the head of the serpent once and for all. He will destroy evil, death will no longer reign, sin, sickness and pain will be eradicated finally and permanently. Although Jesus came the first time as the Suffering Servant, he will come the second time as the Conquering King.

One of the most popular Christmas songs is the great hymn "Joy to the World." Yet when Isaac Watts penned this hymn almost three hundred years ago, the focus was primarily on Christ's second coming, and not—as we may assume—on the incarnation or Christmas celebration. Verses one, two, and four proclaim the joy of all creation at the coming of the King, while verse three celebrates the ultimate defeat of the curse. As you read through this song, consider the hope we anticipate.

Joy to the world! The Lord is come;
Let earth receive her king;
Let every heart prepare him room,
And heaven and nature sing,
And heaven and nature sing,
And heaven, and heaven,
    and nature sing.

Joy to the earth! the savior reigns;
Let men their songs employ;
While fields and floods,
    rocks, hills, and plains
Repeat the sounding joy,
Repeat the sounding joy,
Repeat, repeat the sounding joy.

No more let sins and sorrows grow,
Nor thorns infest the ground;
He comes to make his blessings flow
Far as the curse is found,
Far as the curse is found,
Far as, far as, the curse is found.

He rules the world with truth and grace,
And makes the nations prove
The glories of his righteousness,
And wonders of his love,
And wonders of his love,
And wonders, wonders, of his love.

***The Bible is the story of God's
work to destroy evil ...***

Chapter 3 Discussion Questions:

1. How was Old Testament sacrifice different from the sacrifices of other religions?

2. We speak of Old Testament sacrifice as being "anticipatory." What does this mean?

3. How can God destroy evil without destroying his people?

4. What practical difference can the expectation of God's future "destruction of evil" make in our lives today?

5. How can this hope cause us to rejoice in God's plan?

4

... restore creation ...

Unfortunately, the Christian faith occasionally comes under attack because "Jesus still hasn't returned." In the minds of those who make this assertion, if Jesus was going to come back, he would have done so already. After all, they argue, it's been two thousand years! If Christianity is real, then the Savior surely would have returned by now. What is he waiting for?

The Promise

This argument, however, is not new. In Peter's second epistle, the apostle discusses this very topic. He asserts that in the last days, scoffers will proclaim, "Where is the promise of his coming? For ever since the fathers fell asleep, all things are continuing as they were from the beginning of creation" (2 Peter 3:4).

In response, Peter launches into a discussion of God's past creation and future restoration. He announces that those who make this claim overlook the fact that the universe was created by God (3:5) and one day will be judged by God (3:7). Peter articulates his point when he states:

> The Lord is not slow to fulfill his promise as you count slowness, but is patient toward you, not wishing that any should perish, but that all should reach repentance (3:9).

His assertion is that one day, Jesus will certainly "fulfill his promise" and return to reign upon the earth.

Be careful not to miss what Peter is saying here, especially concerning this "promise." In this case, context is a wonderful tool. Just a few verses prior, Peter explained his purpose for writing this letter: "That you should *remember the predictions* of the holy prophets and the commandment of the Lord and Savior" (3:2). This letter was written so that Peter could remind his audience of the hope given by the prophets.

As you reflect upon your knowledge of the Old Testament, what promises and predictions were declared about the Messiah's coming? Well for one, Genesis 3:15! As we have been discussing, in Genesis 3:15, God promised that the "Offspring of Woman"—later revealed to be the Messiah—will accomplish three tasks. He will: (1) destroy evil, (2) restore creation, and (3) allow God to dwell with his people forever. Although many other promises are provided throughout the Old Testament, these three aspects of this first promise serve as the basis for them all.

With this in mind, consider again 2 Peter 3:9: "The Lord is not slow to fulfill his promise ..." What is this promise? Given the hope of the Old Testament, this promise is that Jesus will destroy evil, restore creation, and make the way for God to dwell with his people. Peter continues:

> What sort of people ought you to be in lives of holiness and godliness, waiting for and hastening the coming of the day of God, because of which the heavens will be set on fire and dissolved, and the heavenly bodies will melt as they burn! But according to his promise we are waiting for new heavens and a new earth in which righteousness dwells (3:11–13).

Again, we find the key statement "according to his promise," which is the same "promise" of 3:9. In these verses, Peter offers clarity about God's final destruction of evil (that "the heavens will be set on fire and dissolved") as well as God's ultimate restoration of creation ("we are waiting for new heavens and a new earth").

Peter's assertion is that as Christians, we ought to live our lives in a manner distinct from those who do not have this same hope of future restoration. Although we may walk through times of great pain and darkness, we have a hope that will not disappoint. We know that this life is not all there is. We know that our purpose goes far beyond the grave. We know that the best this world can offer pales in comparison to our future home.

Although it is true that "Jesus still hasn't returned," we stand today with the same hope held by Peter some two thousand years ago. Just as countless saints have announced throughout the ages, we too proclaim that "according to his promise we are waiting." And we will keep waiting until he comes.

The Patriarchs' Promise

To properly understand what this restoration entails, it is necessary to return to the book of Genesis. Over the last few chapters, we have spent considerable time working through the implications of Genesis 1–3. But now we need to expand our scope of study to the Patriarchs of Israel.

After Adam and Eve are expelled from the Garden, society crumbles ... fast. All restraints appear to be cast off. Cain slaughters his brother Abel because of a misunderstanding. A wicked individual named Lamech makes history for imitating Cain's murderous plot and bragging about it to his two wives. Genesis 6 records how the Lord "saw that the wickedness of man was great in the earth, and that every intention of the thoughts of his heart was only evil continually" (6:6). The Lord is filled with grief over what has become of his prized humanity.

Yet in this dark and hopeless setting, another individual also named Lamech (5:28-31) reveals that all hope has not been lost. Far from the wicked Lamech (4:19-24), this individual—by the same name—reveals a strong trust in the Lord's promise of Genesis 3:15. When his son Noah is born, Lamech offers a prophecy of God's coming victory over the curse:

> Out of the ground that the Lord has cursed this one shall bring us relief from our work and from the painful toil of our hands (5:29).

Now compare this prophecy of hope to the dreadful curse the Lord gave to Adam just a few chapters prior:

> And to Adam he said ... "Cursed is the ground because of you; in pain you shall eat of it all the days of your life" (3:17).

Each of the three words (1) *ground*, (2) *curse*, and (3) *pain*, are identical in these two passages. This is no accident. This is not a coincidence.

Here, Lamech alludes back to the curse of Genesis 3 to proclaim that through his son Noah, relief will be provided. Now we don't get many more details than this. In fact, this one verse is the only statement we have recorded of Lamech in the entire Bible! However, the implications of Lamech's statement are pointed. Evidently, the Lord revealed to him that through Noah and Noah's descendants (eventually leading to the promised Descendant), relief from the curse would be given. And if the curse is lifted, then creation can finally be restored.

Here's the point: In Genesis 5:29, we find a tantalizingly brief statement that anticipates the curse's removal, and by implication, the defeat of the serpent and the ultimate return of creation to the Genesis 1–2 state.

In the pages of Genesis that follow, we quickly discover that the Lord brings a universal flood upon the earth to give the world a fresh "do over." Although this enables Noah's "righteous" family to re-populate the earth, it isn't long before the wickedness of man rears its ugly head once again.

Genesis 9 records the story of how the righteous Noah plants a vineyard and gets drunk (9:20–21). Something inappropriate happens (9:22), and he ends up pronouncing a curse upon his grandson Canaan. Again, even in a "cleansed" world, the wickedness and sinful heart of man is too great. Society once again begins to crumble.

Abraham's Covenant

Fast forward a few hundred years, and we come to the account of Abraham. We meet Abraham in Genesis 11 while he's still a young man named Abram, living in the city of Ur. The Lord appears to him and commands him to leave his homeland and journey to a country unknown (12:1). The next dozen chapters record the incredible acts of faith demonstrated by Abraham because of his commitment to the Lord.

While we often look to Abraham as a model of perfect faith, it's all too easy to forget that he also makes some serious blunders. He lies about his wife Sarah, calling her his sister so that he doesn't get in trouble with the local king (12:12). He does this not just once, but twice (20:2). Furthermore, Abraham does not initially embrace the Lord's promise that he will have a child. Instead, he takes matters into his own hands by using his wife's servant Hagar as a surrogate mother (16:1–6).

Overall, Abraham isn't exactly the flawless hero we typically learn about in Sunday School. His life was raw and painful. He endured considerable trials. He was often tempted. And he failed—on many occasions. But he was still a man who placed his faith firmly in the Lord and his promises.

Throughout these chapters of Genesis, we learn that Abraham is given a promise that theologians refer to as the "Abrahamic Covenant." While Genesis 15:1–21 is perhaps the central passage, aspects of Abraham's promise are also found in 12:1–3, 7; 13:14–17; 17:1–21; 18:9–19; 22:15–18.

In this covenant, the Lord promises that he will lead Abraham's descendants to a specific fertile land (the "promised land"), he will expand Abraham's descendants to be numerous, he will bring the promised Descendant through Abraham, and he will ultimately bless all nations through the accomplishment of this promised Descendant.[5]

And here's the significance: There is a striking similarity between Abraham's promise and the hope of Genesis 3:15 (and for that matter, Lamech's prophecy). In many ways, Abraham's covenant is a promise to reverse the curse. Immediately after proclaiming that Abraham's descendants will be numerous (in 22:17a), the Lord singles out one specific Descendant.[6]

In Genesis 22:17b–18, Abraham is promised an individual Offspring:

> And your offspring shall possess the gate of his enemies, and in your offspring shall all the nations of the earth by blessed, because you have obeyed my voice.

This individual Descendant will "possess the gate of his enemies." What does this mean? In ancient cultures, the "gate" signified the barrier wall of a city, territory, or kingdom. If an individual "possessed the gate of his enemies," it is assumed that he conquered and defeated his enemy. As such, here the Lord promises that Abraham's Offspring will defeat his enemy.

Again, this sounds strikingly similar to the language of Genesis 3:15. Ultimately, Abraham's expectation can be boiled down to the same three aspects originally given in Genesis 3. The Lord promises that the promised Offspring will: (1) *destroy evil* (defeat the serpent through the Offspring of Abraham—22:17b–18); (2) *restore creation* (bring blessing to all nations—12:3; 22:18); and (3) *allow God to dwell with his people* (dwelling with them forever—17:8). Abraham is given a specific promise concerning his specific situation, and yet the implications reach far beyond his own lifetime.[7]

Let us pause for a moment and consider these implications. I think back to when I was a young boy anticipating the Christmas season. One tradition my parents always included in our holiday festivities was the Advent Calendar. For the twenty-four days leading up to Christmas, my sister and I would wake up early and head to this special wooden calendar. Each day, we'd open a little door to discover a new surprise. Sometimes we'd find a piece of candy, sometimes a couple of coins, sometimes a tiny toy, and on rare occasions, a small scrap of paper with a little note scribbled on it.

To be honest, my favorite discovery was always the small scrap of paper. In it, we'd find a message leading us to another location in our home. Perhaps "under the couch," "on the kitchen table," or "in Dad's office." We'd scurry over to the secret spot, only to find another note leading us to another location! We'd run through this routine a few times until we finally identified the mysterious location of our Advent surprise.

This tradition brings back such fond memories. And I can't help but think how this portrays Abraham's surprise at receiving his promise.

Abraham found himself in the promised line of the Skull-Crushing, Creation-Restoring Descendant; he found himself in the genealogical family tree of the promised Messiah. Yet he had *no idea* where this promise would lead him. He simply went where the Lord directed him. In very many ways, he had the simple faith of a child. Just as my sister and I would seek the reward by running to whichever location our parents told us, Abraham sought the reward by following the leading of his God.

In Genesis 15:6—a verse frequently quoted in the New Testament—the text states that Abraham "believed the Lord, and he counted it to him as righteousness." In other words, Abraham simply trusted the Lord's promised plan, and the Lord mercifully justified him.

If we miss this important truth, we misunderstand the entire book of Genesis. Abraham's faith was in the Lord and in his promised Offspring. Although Abraham would not have been able to identify his name as "Jesus," he certainly knew that this individual would be the Savior and Restorer of all things. Abraham's faith was planted firmly in God's promised restoration.

Today, we look back at the lives of countless saints who have gone before us in humble faith, waiting for the realization of this promise. Just as Adam and Eve, Lamech and Noah, and Abraham and Sarah all longed for the day when God's promised Offspring would restore creation, as Christians, so do we. We stand with the redeemed people of God throughout the ages. By grace alone. Through faith alone.

Introducing New Creation

Throughout the rest of the Old Testament, we discover various glimpses of what new creation entails. Although full discourses on this topic are rare, we are offered many insights about what we can look forward to and anticipate in the coming days. The prophet Isaiah offers perhaps the clearest vision into what this restored creation entails:

> The wolf shall dwell with the lamb, and the leopard shall lie down with the young goat, and the calf and the lion and the fattened calf together; and a little child shall lead them. The cow and the bear shall graze; their young shall lie down together; and the lion shall eat straw like the ox. The nursing child shall play over the hole of the cobra, and the weaned child shall put his hand on the adder's den. They shall not hurt or destroy in all my holy mountain; for the earth shall be full of the knowledge of the Lord as the waters cover the sea (11:6–9).

It should be obvious to anyone that apart from a complete change in nature, the picture Isaiah writes about here is impossible. And that is the point! Isaiah articulates a vision of the future that stands diametrically opposed to all we know and have experienced.

We know that if a wolf and a lamb (or a leopard and a young goat) were to lie down together, one would not survive. While I've seen many a field of cattle, I've never seen calves and bear cubs playing together. It just does not happen. That's not how nature works.

Yet the Lord declares through Isaiah, "They shall not hurt or destroy." In other words, the animals (and for that matter, *anything*) that cause pain and death, will no longer be able to do so. Hurt and pain will be eliminated. Suffering and heartache will be no more. Again, the point is that all this is *impossible* apart from God's drastic and cataclysmic action. Only he—as the Author of creation—has the power to step in and change nature. And all we need to do is read a little further in Isaiah to discover this promise:

> He will swallow up death forever; and the Lord God will wipe away tears from all faces, and the reproach of his people he will take away from all the earth, for the Lord has spoken (25:8).

Again, the hope is that God will destroy death and radically transform the universe to the way it was prior to the curse, to the Genesis 1–2 "very good" state.

Reading further in Isaiah, we find out more about the drastic differences that will occur when the Lord restores creation. For example, the Lord proclaims:

> For behold, I create new heavens and a new earth, and the former things shall not be remembered or come into mind (65:17).

Although this may appear to be new revelation provided by Isaiah, if we have first developed a proper understanding of the hope given in Genesis, we will realize that it is far from new. While the details articulated provide a clearer vision, it is the same hope that is offered. Just as in the Christmas Advent calendar search, new details and instructions are offered, yet the hope of a reward remains the same.

What About Us?

Every now and again, we hear the charge that someone is "too heavenly minded to be of any earthly good." However, I cannot help but think how misinformed such a statement is. Honestly, to be of *any* earthly good, one *must* be rather heavenly minded. One must be focused—as was Abraham and countless other Old Testament saints—upon the plan of God to restore creation to the way it was intended to be. Below, I want to offer two closing thoughts.

First, in the modern church, many Christians have an unnecessary disdain for "end times" and eschatology. In light of past disagreements and debates, as well as numerous diagrams and charts, many have pushed the topic of eschatology to the side. In so doing, they have instead sought to focus on the supposed "more pressing needs" of the church today. However, this is not only unfortunate, but quite detrimental to the health of the church.

In this perspective, books like Revelation are either "taboo" or "too confusing." Since they are assumed to be only future focused, they are simply avoided. This, however, is foolishness. Up to this point in this book, we have not yet once examined a single passage from the book of Revelation, yet we have read numerous eschatological texts. We've spent considerable time examining details in the book of Genesis, all of which may be considered eschatological. More than that, we've seen that the entire hope of the Old Testament is about eschatology; it's all about when God will come, destroy evil, restore creation, and dwell with his people.

My concern is that much of modern Christianity has missed the point. Rather than focusing on the fact that God will make all things new, we've sought to make our own lives better. Rather than leaving judgment to the Lord, we've spent hours fretting over how to respond when things don't go our way. Rather than announcing that this world is not our home, we've built up our investment portfolios and retirement funds. Rather than trusting God amidst trials, we've placed our faith in legislative and judicial protection.

Second, in large part, this misplaced focus is due to our altogether unbiblical and seriously inaccurate view of "heaven." To a significant extent, American Christianity has swallowed the world's view that heaven is an ethereal place in the sky we go to when we die. We assume that we'll spend eternity in the clouds, singing hymns for the next ten thousand years. Some assume that we'll become angels. Others assume we'll end up living forever as bodiless spirits.

Whatever the precise details of one's version of this sad vision, it's widely assumed that we will have nothing to do. We'll lead a boring and predictable existence. There will be no more fun, no more adventure, no more spontaneity. In the end, many of us think about heaven and wish for more of earth. Rather than exclaiming, "Come Lord Jesus, Come," we secretly wish for a bit more time—at least until after our next big vacation or until we see our kids grow up.

One of the most unfortunate misconceptions is that we look forward to "heaven." Although it is certainly true that the moment a believer dies, he enters God's presence in "heaven" (Luke 23:43; 2 Corinthians 5:8; Philippians 1:23), that is not where the Bible teaches we will spend eternity. Rather, we look forward to an "earthly" hope, where we will dwell forever upon the new earth in intimate fellowship with our Creator God.[8]

In contrast to a boring eternal existence in the clouds, as Christians we look forward to a world very much like it is today, just without all the sin, sickness, pain, tears, and heartache. All the good aspects of our lives will be expanded and intensified, as the bad parts vanish. My point is that if neither Lamech, Noah, nor Abraham and his descendants were anticipating a spiritualized other-worldly existence, why should we?

Perhaps one of the most articulate authors who wrote on this issue was C. S. Lewis. In his conclusion to *The Chronicles of Narnia* series, he offers a glimpse of the hope of the new earth. He asserts that the current state of things is but a picture of what is to come:

> "Listen, Peter. When Aslan said you could never go back to Narnia, he meant the Narnia you were thinking of. But that was not the real Narnia. That had a beginning and an end. It was only a shadow or a copy of the real Narnia which has always been here and always will be here: just as our own world, England and all, is only a shadow or copy of something in Aslan's real world. You need not mourn over Narnia, Lucy. All of the old Narnia that mattered, all the dear creatures, have been drawn into the real Narnia through the Door. And of course it is different; as different as a real thing is from a shadow or as a waking life is from a dream." ... It was the Unicorn who summed up what everyone was feeling. He stamped his right fore-hoof on the ground and neighed, and then cried: "I have come home at last! This is my real country! I belong here. This is the land I have been looking for all my life, though I never knew it till now. The reason why we

loved the old Narnia is that it sometimes looked a little like this."[9]

I believe Lewis marvelously illustrates the hope for which we long. We yearn to "come home at last!" We long for the day when we will dwell on the earth as it was intended. All joy, all adventure, all excitement, all peace. No sin, no pain, no shame, no tears. For the old order of things will have passed away. Behold, God is making all things new. And in that day, we will no longer refer to it as the "end," but rather, as the "beginning."

The Bible is the story of God's work to destroy evil, restore creation ...

Chapter 4 Discussion Questions:

1. How is Peter's discussion of Christ's return relevant for believers today (2 Peter 3:4, 13)?

2. Based on Genesis 15:6 (in context), what was Abraham's hope?

3. What are some modern misconceptions of what "heaven" will be like?

4. Why is the topic of eschatology (end times) often avoided by Christians?

5. What difference can the hope of God's future "restoration of creation" make in our lives today?

5

... and dwell with his people forever.

In Psalm 73, an individual by the name of Asaph describes his crisis of faith. In this passage, Asaph recounts his experience of doubt and despair in the midst of life's troubles. In so many words, he poses the question: *What's the good in being good?*

Although Asaph begins by recognizing, "Truly God is good to Israel, to those who are pure in heart" (73:1), he quickly transitions to articulate his struggles:

> But as for me, my feet had almost stumbled, my steps had nearly slipped. For I was envious of the arrogant when I saw the prosperity of the wicked (73:2-3).

Just as one easily slips on black ice, Asaph describes how he began to stagger in his faith. He began to envy the ease of life of those who do not follow the Lord. As Asaph watched how unbelievers lived, he began to question why he went to all the effort to serve the Lord.

Asaph describes the situation in pointed terms: Unbelievers have no worries until death (73:4), they don't experience trouble like the believer does (73:5), they eat what they want and they do whatever feels right (73:7), they have no filter—they freely speak whatever comes to mind (73:8), and they don't worry about God's commands (73:10–11). And here we find the exhausted Asaph, serving the Lord with evidently nothing to show for it.

Perhaps you've been there. Maybe you've devoted years to teaching Sunday School, spent countless hours counseling the hurting, and given significant finances to help the needy. Maybe you've resisted temptation longer than you thought possible, held your tongue when you didn't want to, and turned your eyes when it was difficult.

Then tragedy strikes. And you, the believer, the one who has unreservedly honored the Lord by making the hard decisions are left wondering, "God, what's wrong? I've done all you asked of me, and this is what I get?" This is where Asaph finds himself. He states:

> Behold, these are the wicked; always at ease, they increase in riches. All in vain have I kept my heart clean and washed my hands in innocence (73:12–13).

Although at first glance Asaph's response may appear harsh, many of us have likely thought the same thing, haven't we? While we may not pray it out loud or admit to it, deep down we've thought, "All in vain have I kept my heart clean."

Yet we can't stop here, for the psalm certainly doesn't. As Asaph continues, he makes a profound statement:

> But when I thought how to understand
> this, it seemed to me a wearisome task,
> until I went into the sanctuary of God;
> then I discerned their end (73:16–17).

Let me ask you, what is the big deal about the "sanctuary of God"? What was it about this place that caused Asaph's entire disposition to change? Let's think more about what he would have seen.

Upon entrance to the tabernacle, Asaph would have seen the long lines of faithful Israelites. He would have heard the cattle, felt the heat of the fire, smelled the smoke of burning sacrifices, and seen the blood of the animals. It is here that he apparently realizes his foolishness and turns back to the Lord. At this point, we need to consider several of the observations that would have been readily apparent to Asaph in the sanctuary of the Lord.

First, Asaph must have realized afresh the holiness of God. As he gazed upon the numerous animals to be slaughtered, he would have been reminded that no man or woman could approach the Lord's presence without a substitutionary sacrifice. Since God is holy and humanity is inherently sinful, Asaph would have realized that apart from God's mercy, no one could approach his presence.

This need for a sacrifice would have driven Asaph to consider the future of those whom he previously had envied, those *without* a sacrifice. For upon entrance, Asaph declares that he "discerned their end." In other words, he is reminded again of the why he serves the Lord:

> Truly you set them in slippery places;
> you make them fall to ruin. How they
> are destroyed in a moment, swept away
> utterly by terrors! (73:18-19).

No longer does Asaph find himself "slipping," but rather, he realizes that those who reject God have been set in "slippery places." His point is that although committed obedience to the Lord may be difficult—and while rejection of the Lord may appear easy—only those who approach the Lord in humble faith will experience the joy of relationship with him.

In the verses that follow, Asaph describes how he is continually with the Lord (73:23), how he chooses to be guided only by the Lord (73:24), and how he desires to be with the Lord more than anything else this world has to offer (73:25). He then declares:

> For behold, those who are far from you shall perish; you put an end to everyone who is unfaithful to you. But for me it is good to be near God; I have made the Lord God my refuge, that I may tell of all your works (73:27–28).

Although those who reject God will perish, those who humbly approach him by faith will enjoy his presence. Here, Asaph announces his newfound satisfaction of being "near God."

The point of this psalm is that God's presence is to be desired more than anything this world can offer. As Asaph so wonderfully articulates:

> Whom have I in heaven but you? And there is nothing on earth that I desire besides you (73:25).

Yes, this world can certainly offer some incredible experiences. But Asaph's point is that nothing is so good, so refreshing to the soul, so exhilarating to the mind, so fulfilling to the heart, as being in the presence of the Creator God.

The Dwelling Place of God

In what follows, we survey the Bible from Genesis to Revelation as we seek to discover how the theme of God's dwelling place is woven into the very fabric of Scripture's story. In so doing, we discover that from the beginning of creation in Genesis 1, God's plan has always been to dwell with his people in unhindered fellowship.

Garden

In Genesis 1–2, the Lord creates a perfect universe in which he enjoys fellowship and communion with Adam and Eve. As we've seen in the previous chapters, God declares this world "good" in every way imaginable. This earth is carefully crafted to be the residence wherein God dwells among and coexists with his people. In many ways, the Garden is the first temple; it is the location where God walks freely and communicates personally with Adam and Eve apart from any any barriers or sacrifices (3:8). It is not until their sinful rebellion that they are cast from his presence and forbidden to reenter the Garden (3:23–24).

In many ways, the rest of Scripture traces out the intricate and rather complex story of how God will one day defeat evil—ridding humanity of the wretched effects of the curse—and restore creation to the state where he can freely dwell with his people once again.

It is from this brief account in Genesis 1–3 that all of Scripture flows. Again, beginning here, the Lord promises to work in the hearts and lives of mankind throughout history for the purpose of once again dwelling in their midst. Throughout the book of Genesis, the reader is continually faced with this same struggle: *How will God once again dwell with sinful humanity?*

Therefore, as Genesis unfolds, so does God's plan for restoration. It quickly becomes apparent that the hope of the patriarchs is the very same hope first given to Adam and Eve; namely that one day, God will restore his dwelling place with man upon the earth. As such, Genesis concludes lacking a proper ending. It leaves the reader wondering: *When will God finally fulfill his promises?*

Tabernacle

As the Old Testament continues, this prominent hope of Genesis is found to be the same hope of Exodus. The Israelites who lived under Egyptian bondage longed for the day when they would be set free from captivity and allowed to live in their own land, as they were promised in Genesis 15:13–16. In Exodus 2:24, God "remembers" his covenant with Abraham and begins the process of leading the Israelites to their own land.

As the narrative of Exodus unfolds, it quickly becomes clear that for a holy God to dwell amidst a sinful people, strict regulations must be put in place. As such, the primary purpose of the Law (Exodus 20:1–40:38, Leviticus, and Deuteronomy) is to regulate God's dwelling among sinful humanity—for he cannot come in contact with anything profane or unclean.

At this point in the Old Testament storyline, God chooses to take residence in the mobile tabernacle in order to dwell among the Israelites. Consider the detailed instructions concerning this structure (Exodus 25:1–31:11; 35:4–40:38) and the subsequent joy when the glory of the Lord descends upon the tabernacle: "The cloud covered the tent of meeting and the glory of the Lord filled the tabernacle" (40:34).

Ultimately, the book of Exodus ends with the partial realization of what was first promised in Genesis: God dwelling in the midst of his people.

Temple

Eventually, the mobile tabernacle is replaced with the more permanent temple in Jerusalem built by Solomon (1 Kings 5:1–8:66). Yet even that structure does not last. After years of rebellion and disloyalty to the Lord, the Israelites are finally cast into exile (2 Kings 25:1–21), and the glory of the Lord departs from the temple (Ezekiel 10:1–22). The temple is ultimately destroyed (2 Kings 25:13–17; 2 Chronicles 36:19), but all hope is not lost.

The prophets predicted a day when once again, God would dwell in the midst of his people. Only this time, it would last forever. Consider the hope given to the Israelites through the prophet Ezekiel:

> They shall dwell in the land that I gave to my servant Jacob, where your fathers lived. They ... shall dwell there forever. ... And I will set them in their land and multiply them, and will set my sanctuary in their midst forevermore. My dwelling place shall be with them, and I will be their God, and they shall be my people (37:25–27).[10]

What is pointedly evident from this text is that Ezekiel longed for the day when God would once again dwell with his people in restored creation. Clearly, there is an eschatological expectation in the Old Testament that God would eventually dwell in the midst of his people in reconciled relationship forever. This expectation—*God's people dwelling in God's land*—is not unique to any of the Old Testament books, but rather, is one of the central unifying themes that runs throughout.

Christ

The hope of God eventually dwelling with his people in restored creation does not end in the Old Testament. In fact, it is the central hope that forms the foundation and basis of the New Testament's eschatological anticipation. It is into this expectation that Jesus is born. The apostle John writes at the beginning of his Gospel:

> And the Word became flesh and dwelt among us, and we have seen his glory, glory as of the only Son from the Father, full of grace and truth (1:14).

What makes Jesus' birth so very unique is that at the incarnation, God became man. In other words, Jesus became the temple through whom God could fellowship with mankind. Jesus became man so that he could relate to humanity. Yet in so doing, he remained unstained from sin and was thereby able to maintain perfect fellowship with God the Father.

This concept becomes even more pronounced as John's Gospel continues. Upon entering the temple grounds and witnessing the corruption within, Jesus overturns the tables and proclaims, "Take these things away; do not make my Father's house a house of trade" (2:16). When the Jews question him about his actions, Jesus announces, "Destroy this temple, and in three days I will raise it up" (2:19). Then, when the Jews respond that it took forty-six years to build the temple, the apostle John offers key commentary: "But he was speaking about the temple of his body" (2:21).

By becoming the temple, Jesus became the one through whom man could approach God. This theme is developed throughout the New Testament, and it serves as the basis for the next phase in history, the church.

Church

As the body of Christ (1 Corinthians 12:27), the church includes all those who have by faith placed their trust in God's promised Savior—Jesus Christ—for the forgiveness of their sins. As such, each believer is able to approach God through the ministry of Jesus, the promised Savior.

On several occasions, the apostle Paul develops the concept that the church is now the spiritual temple through which man can relate to God through Jesus. In his letter to the Ephesians, Paul states:

> So then you are no longer strangers and aliens, but you are fellow citizens with the saints and members of the household of God, built on the foundation of the apostles and prophets, Christ Jesus himself being the cornerstone, in whom the whole structure, being joined together, grows into a holy temple in the Lord. In him you also are being built together into a dwelling place for God by the Spirit (2:19-22).

Paul doesn't just compare the church to the Jerusalem temple. No, he declares that the church *is* the temple wherein God spiritually dwells among his people.[11] There is no longer a need to travel three times a year to the temple mount to offer bulls and goats as sacrifices.

From this reality, we can develop two primary observations: (1) the church functionally replaced the prior temple—and as such, serves as the spiritual temple for this current age; and (2) the church serves as a picture of God's ultimate eschatological plan for salvation. Just as the tabernacle and temple of the past pictured God's future restored creation, the church—as God's spiritual temple—pictures the hope that sin will eventually be eliminated. In other words, when the church is doing what it is supposed to do, it illustrates the world as God intended it to be.

Here is the point: The very best parts of the church—loving sacrificially, serving faithfully, giving generously, dying to self daily, pressing toward the goal firmly—point to something greater. They point to the ultimate hope that one day, God will undo the curse, remove the effects of sin, restore creation, and ultimately allow man to dwell freely with him in perfect relationship.

Garden-City

In Revelation 21 and 22, the apostle John describes his vision of what the ultimate new earth will look like. Although this vision articulates a restored garden—similar to Eden—this garden is also a city, filled with people from every tribe and tongue and nation. It is this Garden-City that the entire Bible points to and anticipates. Here, God will dwell in unhindered fellowship with his redeemed people from throughout the ages.

Perhaps one of the most striking verses in this passage is Revelation 21:22, which states, "And I saw no temple in the city, for its temple is the Lord God the Almighty and the Lamb." This is nothing short of incredible. Since the fall in Genesis 3, God's fellowship with his people has always been partial; barriers were always necessary, regulations were always in place. But now, God is able to restore the world to what it was designed to be in Genesis 1–2. No more curse, no more sin, no more rebellion, no more suffering, and no more tears.

God's plan from the very beginning was to create a world where he could eventually fill all his creation with his perfect presence. Although this is impossible in the current sin-filled, idolatrous, and rebellious world, it is the hope to which all Scripture testifies. Throughout history, God has certainly revealed his holy presence in various ways at various times. Yet we long for the day when God will restore the world to the way it was intended and dwell among his people in perfect communion and fellowship.

What About Everyone Else?

And here comes the difficult part. If only the redeemed people of God will enjoy this eternal fellowship with their Creator, what about everyone else? What about the people who have chosen to follow their own passions and pursuits to the neglect of the Creator? If we are to truly consider our own eternal destiny, we ought to also wrestle with the implications of the eternal destiny of others. Rather than attempt to survey the entire doctrine of hell, we will focus on one central question: *If God is so concerned about his people, why send some to hell?*

Unfortunately, some who have claimed the title "Christian" have embraced the concept of an angry and vindictive God. In so doing, these individuals have preached a doctrine of hell and damnation with no sorrow in their hearts nor tears in their eyes. They have happily proclaimed that all but themselves are doomed, while self-righteously justifying their own selfish behavior. This is nothing short of sickening. May that never be characteristic of us.

As the Bible records, "Have I any pleasure in the death of the wicked, declares the Lord God, and not rather that he should turn from his way and live?" (Ezekiel 18:23). The Lord is merciful and does not desire that any should perish, but that all would come to repentance (2 Peter 3:9). Yet we cannot let the foolishness of these individuals cause us to neglect the clear teaching of Scripture. For if we minimize the doctrine of God's eternal judgment, we inevitably reject the very heart of the gospel—the substitutionary atonement, the victory of Christ, the redeeming love of the Lord, and the gospel of salvation from sin.

Although much can be said about how the doctrine of hell reveals the righteousness of God's judgment, the holiness of God's perfection, and the justice of God's declaration, perhaps most simply stated, it is a choice. *Hell is a choice.*

God judges no one who truly seeks him. He rejects no one who humbly comes unto him. He turns away no one who approaches him. In fact, he stands at the door and knocks, waiting for unbelievers to come to him (Revelation 3:20). Yet those who willingly choose to reject him, he also will reject. This is crucial for us to consider. If over the course of his entire life, a man chooses to reject God, flee from his presence, and rebel against his commands, then he has already chosen his own destiny.

Perhaps J. I Packer summarizes this concept best in his book *Knowing God*. When Packer discusses the horrors of hell, he states:

> These things are, no doubt, unimaginably dreadful ... But they are not arbitrary inflictions; they represent, rather a conscious growing into the state in which one has chosen to be. The unbeliever has preferred to be by himself, without God, defying God, having God against him, and he shall have his preference. Nobody stands under the wrath

> of God except those who have chosen to do so. The essence of God's action in wrath is to give men what they choose, in all its implications: nothing more, and equally nothing less.[12]

We have seemingly forgotten that God simply "gives men what they choose." Yes, God will certainly judge sin, but he prohibits none from coming to him. And here is the problem, just as we have misplaced the focus from new creation to heaven, we have incidentally also misplaced the focus of hell.

Many have mistakenly built the concept that God rewards those who do right by sending them to heaven, and that God judges those who do wrong by sending them to hell. In so doing, they have ended up with a Santa-Claus-like deity who simply repays each person based upon whether they've been naughty or nice. Please understand, that could not be further from the truth! Again, we must return to the central point of this chapter: *God wants to dwell with his people.*

Let us pause for a moment and consider this incredible truth. God knows every single thing you've done. He knows your deepest darkest secrets. He is aware of each act of rebellion against him. He is familiar with your failures and your successes, your victories, and your defeats. All this, and he still wants a relationship with you; he still longs to call you his child.

Here's the point. We are all guilty. We have all rejected God. We all deserve hell. But thanks be to God for sending his Son Jesus to die in our place. In spite of the punishment we deserve, God freely justifies all who call upon the name of Jesus Christ. In the end, hell is quite simply eternal existence apart from God. Those who choose to dwell with God through Jesus, he welcomes with open arms. Yet those who reject Jesus are rejected by the Father. For they have not approached him through the only sufficient Sacrifice.

We find ourselves at a crossroads, just as Asaph did some three thousand years ago. He weighed the scale with eternal fellowship with God on one side and eternal separation from him on the other.

Ultimately, we are left with the same decision—will we, or will we not pursue God? Will we trust his promise? Will we believe that he will one day destroy evil, restore creation, and dwell with us forever? The choice is yours.

The Bible is the story of God's work to destroy evil, restore creation, and dwell with his people forever.

Chapter 5 Discussion Questions:

1. How does the concept of God's dwelling place form the basis of the Bible's storyline?

2. How did the tabernacle and temple serve to point the Israelites to restored creation?

3. How does the Church picture God's future restored creation (new heavens and new earth)?

4. How can we follow Asaph's example and find encouragement in reflecting on the "sanctuary of God" (Psalm 73:17)?

5. What difference can the hope of God's future "dwelling with his people forever" make in our lives today?

6

So What?

For us this is the end of all the stories, and we can most truly say that they all lived happily ever after. But for them it was only the beginning of the real story. All their life in this world and all their adventures in Narnia had only been the cover and the title page: now at last they were beginning Chapter One of the Great Story which no one on earth has read: which goes on for ever: in which every chapter is better than the one before.
C. S. Lewis, *The Last Battle*[13]

The biblical authors often discussed how knowledge, by itself, is worthless. I could not agree more. At this point, we have worked our way through thousands of years of history, surveyed the promises of God from throughout the ages, considered the hope of the saints through millennia, and examined the single unifying message of Scripture. Overall, we've sought to answer the question: *What is the Bible?*

My hope is that we've answered that question: *The Bible is the story of God's work to destroy evil, restore creation, and dwell with his people forever.*

Now we turn to an equally pressing question: *So what?* What does all this mean for me? Why does it matter? How does this impact you? What difference does this unified message have for each of us?

I want to offer several concluding thoughts for application. While these are certainly relevant for both the Christian and the non-Christian, my goal is to articulate the difference this hope makes for those who embrace God's story as their story. To do this, it is necessary to consider one final passage of Scripture, Hebrews 11.

By Faith

Hebrews 11 has often been referred to as the "Hall of Faith." This passage describes how God's redeemed people lived out their faith in radical obedience to the Lord. What I have always found striking about this passage is the unity of the faith described.

At the start of this passage, "faith" is defined: "Now faith is the assurance of things hoped for, the conviction of things not seen" (11:1). The passage surveys individuals—many of whom we have already examined earlier—and their actions. It describes how "by faith" Abel offered an acceptable sacrifice, "by faith" Enoch pleased God, "by faith" Noah constructed the ark, and "by faith" Abraham left his homeland for a country unknown. Consider the reason for Abraham's faith:

> By faith he went to live in the land of promise, as in a foreign land, living

> in tents with Isaac and Jacob, heirs with him of the same promise. For he was looking forward to the city that has foundations, whose designer and builder is God (11:9-10).

In other words, Abraham lived a nomadic life, trusting that one day God would lead him to the city of hope, the restored city of God, the new earth, the land of promise.

As the passage continues, it describes many others who lived lives faithfully devoted to the Lord—individuals such as Sarah, Isaac, Jacob, Moses, the Israelites who crossed the Red Sea, Rahab, Gideon, Barak, Samson, Jephthah, David, and Samuel. Yet another commonality exists about each of these individuals:

> These all died in faith, not having received the things promised, but having seen them and greeted them from afar, and having acknowledged that they were strangers and exiles on the earth. For people who speak thus make it clear that they are seeking a homeland. If they had been thinking of that land from which they had gone out, they would have had opportunity to return. But as it is, they desire a better country, that is, a heavenly one. Therefore God

> is not ashamed to be called their God,
> for he has prepared for them a city
> (11:13–16).

All these individuals lived as "strangers and exiles." They claimed the promise—they knew that one day, God would destroy evil, restore creation, and dwell with his people—but they did not live to see that day.

Now I want us to pause for a brief moment and return to the beginning of this passage. Since we are now aware of the direction and purpose of Hebrews 11, I want us to consider how the author develops his thoughts to articulate a specific point.

As mentioned above, the first two individuals referenced are Abel and Enoch (11:4–5). Both of these men lived "by faith," both longed for the same promise, and both trusted in the Lord. Yet their lives ended in dramatically different ways: Abel was murdered by his brother. Enoch never died, but was taken to be with God.

There could not be a starker contrast. Abel paid the ultimate price for his faith, while Enoch never had to endure his own death. They both lived "by faith" but each faced incredibly different circumstances.

And it does not take long to trace out this same theme through the rest of the chapter, especially towards the end:

> Through faith [some] conquered kingdoms, enforced justice, obtained promises, stopped the mouths of lions, quenched the power of fire, escaped the edge of the sword, were made strong out of weakness, became mighty in war, put foreign armies to flight (11:33–34).

And what about the others?

> Some were tortured, refusing to accept release, so that they might rise again to a better life. Others suffered mocking and flogging, and even chains and imprisonment. They were stoned, they were sawn in two, they were killed with the sword. They went about in skins of sheep and goats, destitute, afflicted, mistreated (11:35–37).

In other words, "by faith" some accomplished incredible feats, while "by faith" others suffered and died.

Where Do We Go From Here?

Perhaps you have lived a life of ease and comfort. Perhaps you grew up in a Christian family where the gospel was taught, mercy was shown, and grace was offered. Perhaps you attended church each Sunday and received Christ at a young age. Perhaps you were spared the grief of painful betrayal and rejection. Perhaps you were led away from temptation and away from the far-reaching effects of brutal sin.

Or maybe you weren't. Maybe you grew up in a broken family that never darkened the doors of a church. Maybe the Spirit did not convict you of your sins and draw you unto Christ until later in life. Maybe you have deep scars and painful wounds. Maybe you look back at your past and say, "I've wasted so much time." Or perhaps you have not even trusted Jesus Christ as your Savior.

Wherever you are, let me tell you, God has led you there. The God who allows no accidents and makes no mistakes has placed you exactly where you are for a very special purpose. And no matter the trials you have faced or will face, God will guide you. Whatever your circumstances may be, in view of the countless saints who have lived "by faith" before us, the book of Hebrews provides the perfect application:

> Therefore, since we are surrounded by so great a cloud of witnesses, let us also lay aside every weight, and sin which clings so closely, and let us run with endurance the race that is set before us, looking to Jesus, the founder and perfecter of our faith, who for the joy that was set before him endured the cross, despising the shame, and is seated at

the right hand of the throne of God (12:1–2).

Whether we live in New York or Nuremberg, Moscow or Madrid, Berlin or Bangkok, Cape Town or Cairo, for those of us who trust in Christ, our hope is the same. We live by faith. We fight sin because our Savior defeated death, we show kindness because our God lavished mercy upon us, and we weep with the hurting because we long for the day when God will wipe away all our tears.

Wherever you find yourself, I plead with you to trust God's promise and to embrace Scripture as the story into which your life perfectly fits. As we look to Hebrews 11, it becomes clear that embracing the Bible as "our story" enables us to fight sin, live faithfully, and follow Jesus. Although none of the individuals mentioned in this passage lived a perfect life, they all lived "by faith."

That's what is so incredible about the Christian faith. We long for the day when God will finally destroy evil, restore creation, and dwell with his people. On that day, we will stand together with the redeemed people of God from throughout the ages and rejoice in the fulfillment of God's eternal plan.

We'll look around and see countless individuals—some whom we know, many of whom we've heard, and even more of whom we've never heard. We'll glance around and exclaim, "That woman left all to teach in a foreign country! That man planted a church in a difficult city! He was my Sunday School teacher. She led me to Christ. He lived faithfully, even when his life crumbled. She devoted her investments to serve the poor."

I recall the testimony of a student I had in class. The student shared their family's experience living in a largely Islamic country. Because of their Christian faith, the family was robbed and forbidden to share the gospel. They were told that if they continued to talk about Jesus, their well water would be poisoned and they would be killed.

What did this family do in response? Did they give up? Did they hide their allegiance to Jesus Christ? No, they took refuge in the promises of God and did not let fear rule over them. They stood firm in their hope and continued "by faith" to proclaim the gospel lovingly to their community.

Again, where do we go from here? My hope is that as you approach the Bible and seek to know its Author, you will continually recognize the crucial difference that it makes in every situation of life. My hope is that just as the saints of Hebrews 11 lived "by faith," so may we be known as those who live "by faith" and trust in the Lord's promise each moment of every day.

Paradise Restored ... Forever

For those who are believers in Jesus Christ, we long for the day when our faith will be made sight and

SO WHAT?

we will at last gaze upon the Lord in all his holiness and majesty. We yearn for the restoration of creation as promised throughout Scripture and we eagerly anticipate the fulfillment of Revelation 21:1-4:

> Then I saw a new heaven and a new earth, for the first heaven and the first earth had passed away, and the sea was no more. And I saw the holy city, new Jerusalem, coming down out of heaven from God, prepared as a bride adorned for her husband. And I heard a loud voice from the throne saying, "Behold, the dwelling place of God is with man. He will dwell with them, and they will be his people, and God himself will be with them as their God. He will wipe away every tear from their eyes, and death shall be no more, neither shall there be mourning, nor crying, nor pain anymore, for the former things have passed away."

Although the details have been progressively revealed from Genesis to Revelation, we stand side by side with the countless saints who have gone before us, exclaiming, "Come Lord Jesus, come!"

Chapter 6 Discussion Questions:

1. What does it mean to live "by faith"?

2. How can we better incorporate the overarching hope of Scripture in the presentation of our faith?

3. How can we seek to present the many stories of Scripture in relation to the overarching story of Scripture?

4. How is our faith similar to that of the believers described in Hebrews 11?

5. What difference does it make for us to view the Bible as "the story of God's work to destroy evil, restore creation, and dwell with his people forever"?

Endnotes

1. Statistics from "State of the Bible 2021: Five Key Findings," May 19, 2021. https://www.barna.com/research/sotb-2021/. Accessed June 15, 2021.

2. C. John Collins describes the serpent as the "mouthpiece of a Dark Power" (Genesis 1-4: A Linguistic, Literary, and Theological Commentary [Phillipsburg: P&R Publishing, 2006], 156) and concludes by referring to it as the "Evil One" (176).

3. Martin Luther, Luther's Works: Lectures on Genesis, Jaroslav Pelikan, ed.; George V. Schick, trans., vol. 1 (St. Louis: Concordia Publishing House, 1958), 197. Luther also states, "Adam and Eve were encouraged by this promise. Wholeheartedly they grasped the hope of their restoration; and, full of faith, they saw that God cared about their salvation, since He clearly declares that the male Seed of the woman would prostrate this enemy" (193).

4. R. C. Sproul, The Holiness of God. Tyndale: Wheaton, 1986, 45-46.

5. This is most clearly articulated in Genesis 22:17b-18. For further discussion, see T. Desmond Alexander, "Further Observations on the Term 'Seed' in Genesis," Tyndale Bulletin 48:2 (1997): 363-367; and "A Syntactical Note (Genesis 3:15): Is the Woman's Seed Singular or Plural?" Tyndale Bulletin 48:1 (1997): 139-48.

6. The English Standard Version and the King James Version provide the greatest clarity here—versus the New American Standard Bible or New International Version—each of which unfortunately leave the impression that plural descendants are in view here. The Hebrew supports the singular ESV and KJV.

7. For a more thorough discussion on this topic and on Abraham's understanding of the protoevangelium of Genesis 3:15, see Jared M. August, "The Messianic Hope of Genesis:

The Protoevangelium and Patriarchal Promises," Themelios 42:1 (2017): 46-62.

8. For an excellent discussion on this topic, see Randy Alcorn, Heaven (Carol Stream, IL: Tyndale, 2004).

9. C. S. Lewis, The Chronicles of Narnia: The Last Battle (New York: HarperTrophy, 1994), 194-196. Originally published by Collier, 1956.

10. Also worth considering is Ezekiel's reference to the garden of Eden in 36:35, "This land that was desolate has become like the garden of Eden ..." The perfect state of Genesis 1-2 is certainly on the mind of the prophet as he foretells the hope expected for the future. Also note the prophet Isaiah's reference to the garden of Eden in Isaiah 51:3, "For the Lord comforts Zion ... and makes her wilderness like Eden, her desert like the garden of the Lord."

11. Compare this concept of the church as the temple with Jesus' statement in the Gospel of John: "The hour is coming when neither on this mountain nor in Jerusalem will you worship the Father ... The hour is coming, and is now here, when the true worshipers will worship the Father in spirit and truth, for the Father is seeking such people to worship him" (John 4:21, 23).

12. J. I. Packer, Knowing God (Downers Grove: InterVarsity, 1993). Originally published in 1973.

13. C. S. Lewis, The Chronicles of Narnia: The Last Battle (New York: HarperTrophy, 1994), 210-11. Originally published by Collier, 1956.

Also available from
NORTHEASTERN BAPTIST PRESS

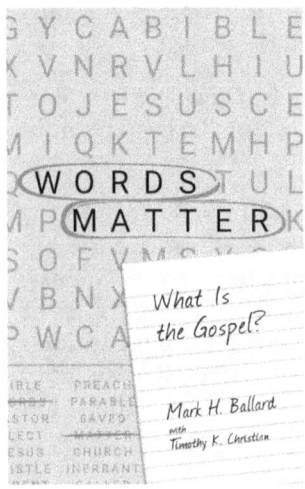

WORDS MATTER:
WHAT IS THE GOSPEL?

Words matter. How we use them and define them determines how we understand the world and how others understand us. In *Words Matter: What Is the Gospel?* Drs. Mark H. Ballard and Timothy K. Christian explore how our personal definition of the word "Gospel" fundamentally affects our view of the world, our lives, and our standing with God.

SCRIPTURE'S STORY:
A UNIFYING HOPE

At the heart of God's story is the hope that all things lost to man will one day be made new.

The Bible presents a single narrative that begins in Genesis and ends in Revelation. Although the sixty-six books that make up the Bible are undoubtedly diverse, they all testify in unique ways to the working out of God's redemptive plan. *Scripture's Story* proposes that every book of the Bible testifies of the coming day when God's promised Offspring will destroy evil, restore creation, and dwell with his people forever. It is this unifying hope that forms the basis of the faith of all believers throughout the ages.

www.ingramcontent.com/pod-product-compliance
Lightning Source LLC
Chambersburg PA
CBHW071420070526
44578CB00003B/638